BABCOCK
FAMILY HISTORY

BABCOCK
FAMILY HISTORY
(England-USA-Canada)

ALBERT BABCOCK

CITI OF
BOOKS

CITIOFBOOKS, INC.
3736 Eubank NE Suite A1
Albuquerque, NM 87111-3579
www.citiofbooks.com
Hotline: 1 (877) 389-2759
Fax: 1 (505) 930-7244

Ordering Information:
Quantity sales. Special discounts are available on quantity purchases by corporations, associations, and others. For details, contact the publisher at the address above.

Printed in the United States of America.

ISBN-13:	Softcover	979-8-89391-347-7
	eBook	979-8-89391-348-4

Library of Congress Control Number: 2024919363

BABCOCK FAMILY HISTORY

ENGLAND:

The Babcock Families in America and Canada can trace their origins to England to the twelfth century and probably a Saxon origin. The Babcock family in England spelled their name Badcock: probably pronounced "Badco". The name was changed in America after many misspellings by magistrates (Badcock, Badcooke, Badcocke and Badcook) to name a few. It finally became Babcock about 1680 when it was spelled that way in the Probate records of John Badcock's estate.

There is some evidence of the family presence in Wivenhoe, Essex County near the sea. Wright's History of Essex makes reference to the Badcock Mansion that was occupied by Sir Richard. There is come assertion that the Badcock family may have been founded A.D. 449 by a Saxon warrior in the ranks of Hengist and Horsa, who came with a Saxon army to help the English against the Picts and Scots.

"Family tradition" has it that a younger brother of Sir Richard Badcock lived at Wivenhoe, Essex, England-born about 1580-named James Badcock, a clergyman of the Church of England, of Puritanical persuasion, who became an exile in 1620 to Leyden, Holland, for the sake of religious liberty, and sailed from there, with others to New England. He has been said to have sailed on the Queen Ann arriving at Plymouth, MA in 1623. There is no documentation to support this connection. He more likely arrived at Portsmouth, R.1. about 1640. Records show that James Badcock was living in Portsmouth, R.1. in 1642

The solid ground of fact, therefore, upon which at last we stand may be indicated in about two words.: 1. Our branch of the Babcock folk came from old England to New England early in the seventeenth century-certainly prior to 1642. 2. We share with the English Badcocks a coat of arms which helps to show that, as a family, we have lived long enough in the world to know how to live wisely and, therefore well.*.

Subject: Miranda Grant…mother of Albert Berton Babcock.. grandmother of Mervin Babcock..great mother of Lorne

Name:	Miranda Grant	
Age:	16	
Estimated Birth Year:	abt 1834	
Birth Place:	New York	
Gender:	Female	
Home in 1950:	Kingsbury, Washington, New York\	
Family Number:	14	

Name	Age
Billing Grant	39
Water Grant	14
Benoni Grant	12
William Grant	5
George Grant	1
Elisa Grant	39
Caroline Grant	20
Mary Grant	17
Miranda Grant	16
Lois Grant	10
Elizabeth Grant	8
Phebe Ann Grant	3
Susan Grant	5

Household Members: (Caroline Grant through Susan Grant)

Your grandmother and grandfather. Your father George. Fides passed away in USA before the family came to Canada. Mervin is my father. I always thought we were Englis, and I still think so but there is the info entered at that time.

Subject: 1916 Sask Census

Name:	Mervin Babcock
Gender:	Male
Marital Status	Single
Age:	2
Estimated Birth Year::	1914
Birth Place:	Saskatchewan
Home in 1916:	Saskatchewan, Prince Albert, 21
Address:	47, 19, 2, Weldon
Racial or Tribal Origin:	Scotch
Relation to head of Household:	Son

Name	Age
Bert Babcock	45
Edith Babcock	41
George P. Babcock	22
Fildes Babcock	20
Household Members: Goldie Babcock	18
Lillie Babcock	11
Lilace Babcock	9
Isebla Babcock	7
Eva Babcock	4
Mervin Babcock	2

Horace Everett Babcock was the last one born in 1917-2006

This is our great, great grandfather. You will see a Joseph above Charley. That is our great grandfather and he is the father of our grandfather Albert(Birt) Babcock.

Subject: 1870 New Berlin, Waukesha, Wisconsin

Name:	Joseph Babcock
Estimated Birth Year:	abt 1832
Age in 1870:	38
Birth Place:	Indiana
Home in 1870:	New Berlin, Waukesha, Wisconsin
Race:	White
Gender:	Male
Value of real estate:	View image
Post Office:	Waukesha

Name	Age
Joseph Babcock	38
Miranda Babcock	36
Sarah Babcock	15
Rachel Babcock	18
Lois Babcock	12
Burnis Babcock	8
Joseph Babcock	5
Charley Babcock	3

Household Members:

Lorne Everett Babcock (born Aug 20, 1941, Melfort, Sask) MARRIED Caroline Jean Coe (born Jan 22, 1942, Hudson Bay Junction, Sask) in 1960 at Melfort, Sask

Mervin Harold Babcock (born June 8, 1914, Melfort, Sask) married Margaret Jensen (born 1917, Kinistino area, Sask) in 1940/41

Albert Babcock (born Nov 1871/71, Muskego, Waukesha Co, Wisconsin-died Melfort, Sask) married Edith May Schultz (born May 1875, Boone, Iowa-died Regina, Sask) in Muskego, Waukesha Co, Wisconsin, Albert was 21, Edith was i6. Albert & Eda both died at the age of 84 yrs.

George Pardon born Aug 8, 1893, Muskego, WS
Matilda Miranda born Oct 1895, Muskego, WS
Goldie Gwendolin born Feb 28, 1898, Muskego, WS
Sherman Gordon born Mar 1900, Muskego, WS
Sylvia born 1901, Mauston, WS
Lilian Albertan was born Oct 1903, Mauston, WS
Liela Belle born Mar 1907, Mauston, WS
Isabelle April born Apr 19,1909 at Rosco, South Dakota
Evangeline Victoria born Dec 29, 1911, Melfort, Sask
Mervin Harold born June 8, 1914, Melfort, Sask
Horace Everett born Dec 30, 1917 on NW 35-47-19-W2

1895...Summit, Juneau, Wisconsin..
1900.. Summit, Juneau, Wisconsin
1910.. Bjornson, McHenry, North Dakota
1911..Saskatchewan

Joseph Pardon Babcock (born Sep 1832, Boon Twp, Harrison Co, Indiana-died Oct 5, 1901, Mauston, Juneau Co, Wisconsin) married Miranda W. Grant (born Dec 1834, Fort Edward, Washington Co, New York-died Feb 3, 1905, Juneau Co. Wisconsin) on Apr 5, 1853 in Waukesha Co, Wisconsin

1860..Muskego, Waukesha, Wisconsin
1870..New Berlin, Waukesha, Wisconsin
1880..New Belin, Waukesha, Wisconsin
1900..Summit, Junea, Wisconsin

Children of Miranda W Grant and Joseph Pardon Babcock are:
Sarah born abt 1855
Rachel born 18 Oct 1857-died 10 Oct 1946
Lois born Feb 1860
Barnis born 4 Dec 1861
Joseph born 4 Dec 1863
Charles Billing born 9 Feb 1866-died 1955
Albert born Nov 1871
George born Apr 1874
James M. born Jun 1876

James R. Babcock (born 1803, Westfield, Washington Co, New York) married Rachel Phebe Mulkins (born abt 1810, Vermont) on 26 Dec 1822 in Posey Twp, Harrison Co, Indiana, the daughter of Henry Mulkins (born 1775, Mass-died ber Oct 5. 1940, near Charlestown, Clark Co, Indiana)

Abigail A. Babcock b: ABT 1830 IN Vermont -died 1908
Joseph Pardon Babcock b: 8 SEP 1832 in Boon Twp., Harrison Co., IN
Augustus James Babcock b: ABT 1843 in Wisconsin

1850..Koshkonon, Jefferson Co, Wisconsin
1860..Koshkonong, Jefferson C0, Wisconsin

Sherman Babcock (born Oct 19, 1762, South Kingston, Washington Co, Rhode Island-died Jan 18, 1851, Westchester Clark Co, Missouri) married Delecta Rich (born 1771, Washington Co, New York-died btw Feb 1847 & June 1850, Missouri) in 1788 in Westfield, Washington Co, New York

In 1850, Sherman lives with his son Pardon Babcock in Benton, Knox County, Missouri. He is 87, a revolutionary soldier who was born in Rhode Island.

Story about Sherman on Ancestry.com

Like many others I have been actively searching for the parentage of South Kingston-native Sherman Babcock 1762-1851, pursuing many dead-end leads over the years, and even narrowing down through the painfully show process of elimination which branches of Babcock family of South Kingston and its environs he could be descended from. The more evidence I gather the more my focus becomes narrowed onto one couple in particular – which is also the couple that has been the most obvious choice from the beginning for onomastic reasons: that couple being Job Babcock and Edy Sherman. They originated in South Kingston and by 1784 were living in Colrain, Massachusetts, probably by way of Stonington, Connecticut, where one of Edy's siblings lived at least for a while.

Let's look at the obvious onomastic evidence for a moment. The name Sherman as a surname and as a given name automatically catches the eye. But add to that the usual name lady. Sherman Babcock, and his children obviously had pioneering spirits, scattering all over the western territories as they opened for settlement. In the later decades of his life Sherman near and eventually with his youngest son Panlon Babcock (1814 – 1890). I the 1850 census for Benton Twp.. Knox Co., Missouri, Sherman was listed in Pardon's household. Among Pardon's children was listed a 13-year old daughter named Edy. Once again that extremely unusual name appears. Let's look now at the migratory path this family took in the latter 1700s, Edy (Sherman) Babcock was a legatee in the 1782 will of her father Daniel Sherman of South Kingston, in which she and her husband Job Babcock was listed as living in Colrain, MA. In 1777 and 1778 Sherman Babcock enlisted for military service in Connecticut (1777 in Groton, and 1778 in Stonington).

This matches well the Sherman family migratory path from South Kingston to northwestern Massachusetts via Stinington, Connecticut. After his term of service expired Sherman then settled in 1779 in Pownall, Vermont. Pownall, on the southern edge of Vermont, is just a few miles from Colrain, Massachusetts, where Job and Edy were definitely living in 1784. Overlayed one another, the paths followed by Sherman and Job are nearl identical. But there is more. By 1790 Sherman Babcock had removed to Westfield Twp.. Washington Co., NY. and he and his wife are listed in the 1790 census adjacent to James Rich, almost certainly his wife Delecta's father. There appears to have been something a small migratory push from Colrain to Westfield Twp. about 1781 respected, elder veteran John McCartney of Colrain granted his land in Colrain away and settled in Washington County, NY; and in the 1790 census is also living in Westfield Township as is Sherman Babcock. Perhaps even Job and Edy were part of this migration even at their advanced ages.

Another story about Sherman Babcock

Sherman Babcock, 1762 – 1851

Sherman Babcock was born on 19 Oct 1762 in South Kingstown.. Washington County, Rhode Island. Nothing has been uncovered as to his parentage or siblings. Most of what we know about him and his family comes from certain vital, land, and census records, and information provided in an application for a Revolutionary War pension, Sherman served during the Revolutionary War as a private in the militia of seven states. Sherman enlisted in the Connecticut Militia to serve as a substitute for three months. He served under Captain Joseph Fisa in the 4th Regiment and was stationed in Groton and Stonington Point. CT. On 25 Jun 1777 Sherman again enlisted in the Connecticut Militia to serve for nine months. He served under Captain Josiah Baldwin in Colonel John Ely's regiment. and was stationed in New London, Connecticut. His company was marched to White Plains. NY. in preparation for a crossing, to Long Island, which never happened, though Colonel Ely was captured by the British. Sherman returned to

Stonington Point, and on 14 May 1778 Sherman enlisted for a third term of one year. He served under Captain Joshua Babcock in Colo John Topham's regiment, and was stationed in Tiverton, Rhode Island. After mastering, out, he settled in Pownall, Vermont. While there he was drafted for two consecutive tours of two months, each serving to guard prisoners and maintain the border. He served under Captain Briggs in Colonel Robertson's regiment. He was likely discharged about Apr 1779. By 1789 he was settled in Westfield (later called forth Aun). Washington County, New York (near Lake Champlain). He married Delecta Rich, daughter of James Rich. Sherman became the pastor of the First Baptist Church of Westfield on 12 Feb 1790. In 1790 or 1791, Sherman and Delecta had the first of their eleven children, son Thomas. Another son. Young (also called Youngs) was born in 1792. He served with the First Baptist Church until 1792. The Babcock family then moved to Panton, Addison County, Vermont. Son Barnes (also called Barnabus) was born there on 24 Feb 1794. On 4 July 1794. Sherman helped found the Panton Baptist Church. The family moved back to Westfield sometime after this. Daughter Amanda was born there in 1795, and son Hiram (also called Henry) was born in 1798. On 19 Sep 1799, Sherman was again called to become the pastor of the First Baptist Church of Westfield. He was ordained by a council of churches from Hartford, Queensbury, Sharon, Kingsbury, Granville, and Middletown, Vermont. He served for six years, and permanently serve his connection to the Church on 5 Jn 1805. Sons Lee (also called Stephen) and James R (possible named after his grandfather) were born in Westfield I 1801 and 1803, respectively. The family again returned to Panton before the birth of their eight child, daughter Salome, in 1806. Sherman bought 15 acres of land in Ferrisburg from Ferris Holcomb, which was recorded on 7 Apr 1806. Sen Rowland was born 5 Mar 1809, followed by daughter Elesta (also called Lusty or Linty) in 1812, and son Pardon A… 28 Aug 1814. On Oct 1809, Youngs married Beulah (or Bela) Bishop, oldest daughter of Jesse Bishop, in Panton. Thomas married Clarissa Ferris, daughter of James Ferris, on 20 Feb 1810 in Panton. Barnes was married in 1814 Aseniah Grover, likely in Fort Ann. Thomas served a pilot in the U.S. Naval Squadron on Lake Champlain from 27 Apr 1814 to 28 Nov 1814 (during the War of 1812). Barnes also served during the war, Sherman sold his land in Panton 23 Sep 1814, possibly to escape the fighting. Sometime between 1815 and 1818 he and his family started a migration west that would ultimate end in Oregon. By 1818, Sherman and family were settled in Posey Township, Harrison County, Indiana. More of Sherman's children were married here over then next twenty years, Stephen married Sally Washburn on 2 May 1818 in Clark County, Indiana. Amanda married Jonathan Elsworth 14 days later (on 16 May 1818) in the same country, James married Rachel Mulkins, daughter of Henry Mulkins, on 26 Dec 1822 in Posey, Rowland married Nancy Pyburn, daughter of Richard Pyburn and Mary A Hardin on 22 Oct 1828 in Posey, Eleda married Willard Mulkins (brother of Rachel) on 18 May 1834 in Posey. Pardon married Elizabeth Pyburn (sister of Nancy) on 29 Oct 1835 in Posey. Hiram married Lydia about 1820. No information is known of any marriage of Salome.

In June 1832. Congress passed the Pension Law, which provided pensions for Revolutionary War Veterans. Sherman filed for his pension on 2 Oct 1832 in open court in Harrison County. He was placed on the pension rolls for Indiana {#122333} on 26 Oct 1833 at a semi-annual rate of $10.00, retroactive to 4 Mar 1831.

In 1842 Sherman and Delecta moved to Pleasant Prairie. Racine County {now Kenosha County}. Wisconsin with their sons Rowland and Pardon. Sherman and Delecta were received into the congregation of the First Baptist Church in Kenosha on 18 Sep 1844. In Feb 1847 Sherman and Delecta moved to Benton Township, Knox County, Missouri to be near to their Pardon and his family. It also appears that Rowland moved there briefly as well, as his son Richard was born in Knox County in 1847. Sherman continued his Baptist ministry in Missouri. Records show that he married at lead four couples in Knox County between Apr and now 1848.

Sherman died on 18 Jan 1851 in Winchester, Clay Township, Clark Co, Missouri, 1850 Census records (taken in June 1850) do not mention Delecta: it may be presumed that she died between Feb 1847 and June 1850, probably in Missouri. No burial place has been identified for Sherman or Delecta.

Job Babcock (born abt 1721, Kingston, Washington, Rhode Island-died aft 1775, Kingston, Washington Co, Rhode Island) married Edith Sherman (born Apr 4, 1745, Darmouth, Bristol Co, Mass-died Kingston, Washington Co, Rhode Island) abt 1761, (Edith Sherman was his 2nd wife..marriedwhen she was 16). Job first married Susannah Hopkins who died abt 1760.
Edith's parents were Daniel Sherman & Susannah Earle.

Captain Job Babcock (born abt 1697, South Kingston, Washington Co, Rhode Island-died Mar 1775, South Kingston, Washington Co, Rhode Island) married Mary Elizabeth Hull (born 1698, Kingston, Washington Co, Rhode Island-died 1771) on 10 Oct 1717 in North Kingston, Washington Co, Rhode Island

Job Babcock (born 10 Feb 1669, Westerly, Washington Co, Rhode Island-died 10 Feb 1755, South Kingston, Washington Co, Rhode Island) married Deborah Reynolds (born abt 1647, North <u>Kingston, Washington Co, Rhode Island-died</u> bef 1755, South Kingston, Washington Co, Rhode Island) abt 1695 in Westerly, Washington, Rhode Island

Captain John Babcock (born 1644, Portsmouth, Newport Co, Rhode Island-died 1685, Westerly, Washington Co, Rhode Island) married Mary Lawton (born 1644, Portsmouth, Newport Co, Rhode Island-died 8 Nov 1711, Westerly, Washington, Rhode Island Tradition says that John and his wife, Mary, eloped from Newport, settled upon the east bank of the Pawcatuck River, on Massatuxet Cove (now what is the new Avondale town of Westerly Rhode Island) with no neighbors but the friendly Indians and that they were not discovered by their parents for several years. Muh poetry and romance have been written upon this tradition, but as no history has been found to establish it as a fact, and as authentic records seen clearly to disprove the statement, we must class the elopement story as fiction. John was propounded a freeman of the Colony of Connecticut May 14, 1676, and later was admitted a freeman, John Babcock and his father were members of the Misquamicut Company and went there with the first permanent settlers. At that time John was about eighteen years of age. He received an appointment of land and the same as other settlers. He settled in Westerly on the banks of the Pawcatuck River, near what is now Avondale, RI, and his oldest son. James inherited and occupied the homestead. Some of the homestead land was still occupied by descendants of John in 1903. In 1675 King Philip's War broke out, and most of the pioneers of Westerly were obliged to flee from their homes and take refuge on the Island of Rhode Island. By Sept. and Oct. 1676, they had begun to return to their abandoned lands and to rebuild their ruined houses and barns. The indications are that John Babcock, and his family remained in their home in Westerly, which was across the river from Connecticut, and as he could have no protection from Rhode Island sought the protection of Connecticut. From the time of its settlement, Westerly was claimed by both Rhode Island and Connecticut, and Connecticut did not relinquish her claim to the town until 1728. Traditions says that John volunteered with the Connecticut Militia, which was organized for protection against the Indians: that in King Philips War he was with the Connecticut Militia in the "Great Swamp Fight". Dec. 19,1675, and that his son Elihu was born at that time. After King Philip's War was over, and the white settlers of Westerly had returned to their homes. John Babcock was closed Coactivator of the Peace for Westerly, June 12, 1678. He was Deputy from Westerly to the Colonial Legislature in 1682 and 1684. He died intestate (1685) and a will disposing of the estate was made by the Town Council. The inventory of the personal property amounted to 790 pounds and was the large recorded in the town for many years. By law the oldest son, James, received all the real estate, one half of which he conveyed by deed to his mother. The widow received one third of the personal property, the remaining two thirds being divided equally among the nine younger children.

James Babcock (born 12 Jun 1612, Wivenhoe, Essex, England -died 12 Jun 1679. Portsmouth, Newport Co, Rhode Island) & Sarah Bourne (born 1616, Essex, England-died 1665, Milton, Norfolk Co, Mass) were married 2 1638 in Portsmouth, Newport Co, Rhode Island

James Babcock (born 1580, Wivenhoe, Essex, England-died 12 Jun 1679, Stonington, Norwich Co, Connecticut) & Mary? (born 1584, Wivenhoe, Essex, England-died 1623, Milton, Norfolk Co, Mass) were married abt 1611 in England

CHAPTER I

THE UNBELIEVABLE

It all started in a small town and a farm in Wisconsin, USA. My grandfather had a farm not far from town. They had a mixed farm of dairy cows, horses, OXEN, pigs, chickens.

Grandfather and grandmother had a big family, there were thirteen children in the family at one time. Then an accident happened on the farm. The accident happened to be my dad and his brother playing in an old wash tub on an old pond.

Apparently, the pond was deeper. Then my dad and his brother thought they were in the washtub using it as a boat. They upset the washtub and dad's brother fell out and drowned. Dad could not swim to save his brother. Then there were only twelve children left on the farm.

Grandpa and grandma provide a good living for all the kids they had. They had a big garden, their own meat which was canned. For the garden stuff there was a root cellar used.

Grandpa would plant oats and barley each year for the grain he needed to feed the livestock on the farm. They had about seventy-five head of dairy cows and also a lot of swine.

Grandma and the older children were in charge of milking the cows every day. That was a chore all of its own. There was little playtime for the children because not only chores to do, but they also had homework from the school they attended.

The school they went to was a country school. Grandpa would harness a horse and hitch it up to a wagon in the spring so they could use it to go to school. In the winter they used a bobsleigh for traveling to school.

The reason for the wagon and the bobsleigh was the family was a mixture of boys and girls. There were six boys and seven girls in the family which grandpa and grandma had. Sometimes the children would walk to school. Not very often they would walk to school.

On grandpa's farm and all the rest of the farms around the area there were no balers. This was because of the years in the eighteen hundreds. That meant everything was put up loose in stacks. The oat sheafs were also put in stacks in the farmyard close to the barns.

Grandpa would wake up in the middle of the night. The pig would be squealing in the straw stack of intruder was there.

Of course, the intruder was a black bear that was feeding on the piglets. After the pig settled down a little while grandpa waited for the bear to leave the straw stack and shoot the bear with his shot gun. About a week or so later another bear was in the straw stack.

Grandpa got up and saw movement in the straw stack. He knew it was a bear again, so he took the shot gun and shot the bear in the straw stack and retrieved him the next morning.

He skinned the bear and cut up for meat which was canned and smoked. That was one way to preserve the meat. Grandpa had a problem with bears before they liked pork, I guess, especially the little.

Then one night about midnight grandpa heard a noise from the straw stack again. Grandpa get up and usual shot in the straw stack and kill whatever was moving in the straw stack.

When grandpa woke up the next morning to remove the bear. When grandpa dug out the bear, he thought it was but wasn't a bear. Grandpa went to the house and woke up his son to help him drag the thing out of the straw stack. Then they loaded the thing up in the wagon and hauled out to the field. They dug a hole and buried it.

About a month or two after that grandpa and my dad decided to come to Canada. It was in the early nineteen hundred when they started the homestead in Canada. They had to build a house and fence the land for the livestock.

Then they sent word to grandma to come to homestead in Canada. When grandma got word to come to Canada, she sold the pigs except the ones they butchered and smoked canned.

They butchered a few chickens and canned them for the trip to Canada also. They load up the wagon for the trip to the homestead. The next morning, they gathered up the cattle for the trip.

One of the boys had to harness up horse and oxen and hook up in the wagon for grandma. The rest of the children gathered the cattle for the trip and packed the wagon with clothes and soap which grandma made. They also cook supplies. Then the next thing was to start their journey to Canada to homestead.

When grandma and the kids were on the trail, they used the sun as direction to know where to go. There were no signs to follow just when grandma found in a creek or pond.

That is when they stoped for the first night. The kids would make the cattle circle for them to bed down for the night. I would like to know how to milk all the cattle with no barn or corral to tie them up. Grandma and the kids would make only a few miles a day. The horse and oxen worked very well.

Grandma must have had a hard time not knowing the trail or the wildlife and the natives on the trail. They had hard times on the trail which was to find water for the livestock and fires wood for fires for cooking and a little heat. There was no playing for the kids, just herding cattle on the trail, and collecting wood for fires. So, grandma would use it for cooking.

Now back to the homestead, where grandpa and dad had built a house which was a one room house. Then the chore was to dig a well and crib it in and also to build a root cellar and a chicken cope.

Once the fencing was done, the next project was to get firewood for the winter. Then the next thing was to get hay for the livestock that was coming with grandma and the kids. It was a pretty tight fit for twelve children and two adults to fit in a small one room house. Soon as grandma got there, she was surprised how grandpa and dad had things in place for the livestock and a house built and everything in place.

Grandpa sent dad to the country school in the fall. While dad was in school grandpa would work for neighbors for cook stove and a washing machine. The washing machine was the kind you had to crank by hand. The children took turns pumping the handle to make the washing machine work. Then took turns to bring in the wood for the house.

Grandpa also worked for farmers in exchange for chickens feed for first year. Also, he works for farm machinery like a plow and cultivator. Grandpa broke land so he could seed the land. Grandpa got the land for free while he broke at least ten acres of land a year for crops or planted grass seed for hay.

On the home stead when grandpa and dad built the house, it was built out of one by six and two by fours. Grandpa did a very good job on the house except it did not have any insulation in it. Cardboard boxes were used on the walls split open and hung by can lids nail on the walls. The house had about four windows, all single pane glass. Grandpa would have to keep the fire on all night to keep it warm and keep the water from freezing.

When grandpa made the chicken cope, there was a high bank not far from the house. Grandpa and dad dug out a hole and installed peeled logs as walls and poles for the roof. Then a door was made out of the slabs that was left over from the house. The chicken cope was then buried back with the sand. Then wooden pop boxes filled for straw were used as nests for the hens to lay eggs in. The chickens were let out each morning feed wheat and barley and watered. There were about fifty chickens in the group. Some were for butchers and others were the laying hens.

When grandpa made the chicken cope it was made pests free like from foxes and weasels and skunks. There was no fence made for the chickens, they just roamed free around the house and in front of the chickens' cope. The chickens were not allowed in the garden which was fenced out of short cut slaps.

When grandpa and grandma's children grew up and left home, my dad took over the farm. That was after dad and his brother were done in the second world war. Dad and his older brother were also involved in the world war. In both wars, they worked in the shell factory. In between the wars dad and his brother worked on the homestead. They also worked for different farmers and companies to bring extra money into the homestead.

Eventually, dad left the homestead and went to work in the mine in B.C... That is where he met his wife in a small town at that time.

CHAPTER II
AS THINGS TURN AROUND FOR BETTER

While dad was working in the coal mine, he had to cross a bridge every day to get back and forth to work. Every day he would have to fill his lantern up with coal oil. Then make sure the wick was long enough for his next shift. The camp was a very busy place at shift changes, and at mealtimes.

When dad was working in the coal mine, he dated my mom for about a year or so. In the nineteen fifties, when I was born, dad and mom moved back to grandpa's and grandma's homestead. I do believe they got married before they left B.C... When they left B.C… it was early spring which I was about six-week-old.

My mother had four children before I was born. Dad had an instead family to start out with, and dad had an old Studebaker car to bring the family to the homestead. My brothers and sisters were born on the homestead with a midwife. My oldest sister helped with the delivery of my brothers and sisters. Mom used cotton diaper, which can be washed once a week.

One the homestead one of our chores was to clean out the well in the spring. One spring, there was a new crib to be installed in the well. Each spring there were salamanders in the bottom of the well which were removed.

When I went trapping, my older brother would skin the animals and stretched the hides to sell. So, I got the money for the hides. I caught only weasels in the wintertime. They paid me ten cents a hide, just enough for candy. Dad was scared for us kids one fall when he went hunting the seen a bobcat close by our home. The bobcat was there only about two days and left.

One of chores was to collect wood for the wintertime which was hauled by a maple leaf truck and stock pile in the yard. Dad had on hand fifteen-thirty tractor which was used on an old buzz saw. When they cut the tree into wood blocks, dad would throw the block into a pile away from the work area of the saw.

In the mid-nineteen fifties my uncle who works on the grain elevators came to our place with a truck and trailer of lumber. They built a brand-new home for my dad which was very nice. Dad and mom got the new home with my sisters. The old homestead house was used for us boys to sleep in.

The older brother was responsible for keeping the fire going all night in the fall and wintertime. When our new house was built, my uncle and aunt stayed in a trailer they brought down their place. They also had a small dog that would chase me around the old house and yard in which we were playing.

Shortly after the house was built and my uncle and my aunt left to go back to their home, dad went and bought a couple of goats. One was a Billy goat and the other was a nanny goat. My oldest brother and mom would take turns to milk the nanny goat twice a day. The milk had a bitter taste to it, but we got used to the milk. Mom makes goat cheese from the cream and uses lots of salt in it.

One day I decided to fence the Billy goat in a small pasture. The only thing I could find was a roll of baler twine or binder twine. That process did not work well at all because the Billy goats had a mind of his own. He went through the fence I made like it was not there. I thought I could save the dump goat's life by keeping him in a fence pasture.

Dad would wake up every morning to see the Billy and nanny goats on the car hood and roof. Eventually the goats were tied up at night to keep them from destroying everything in the yard. Then in the fall Billy goat had to put down for our meat which was mixed with deer meat to make hamburger.

My mom had a full-time job looking after us and doing canning all the meat that was brought home from hunting and fishing. There was also canning for when we picked blue berries in the pines. West and North of us when we picked blue berries, dad and mom made a picnic out of it. That gives dad and my oldest brother a chance to go bear hunting in the pines. The bears were plentiful, it did not take dad long and had a bear ready to take back to the homestead. We filled syrup pails of blue berries and dumped them in the washtub. Mom sorted the green ones and leaves out when the syrup pails were emptied.

Then the trip back home in the old maple leaf truck we rode in the box. Mom would always say now to sit down and do not stand up while we are moving. When we arrived back home, mom made supper then off to bed we would go.

The next morning mom would prepare cellars for canning the fruit we picked, and the bear dad had shot. There was no electricity in the houses on the farm. There was a big pail in the well-used fridge and a root cellar for some canning and garden stuff that we grew.

One winter day mom and dad went to town for groceries and my older sister made us promise not to tell on her to make ice cream for us. My sister used a simple recipe, it was canned milk, snow and sugar. The snow had to be dug out of snowbanks because of the slot from the stove pipes. Another treat was the hard sap of the pine trees. We called it pine gum which tasted terrible, which we spit the juice out and never got a sweet taste at all.

When we attended school, we had to go to the country school which was fine but a longer walk. The only school bus was one that took the high school kids to the city. In our school there were two rooms, and the basement was divided into washrooms. The girls had one side, and the other side was for the boys.

In the school the two rooms contain about fifteen students each room in grade six to eight. There was a big wood stove in the basement to heat the school and a water jug for students to drink from with steel cups pails of water in the basement for washing hands and an old towel to dry on.

In the spring sometimes we would catch a ride with a friend of ours which had polio. My older brother would help in the jeep after school and start the jeep up. Our friend's dad had made the jeep for his son out of an old auto frame and installed a wooden deck and fenders out of his plywood. There was only one seat for him, and we could ride on the deck. We would arrive at school one hour early.

Sometimes when we walked to school, we would stop at a farm which had cows, and the lady would give us a glass of milk and cookies as a treat for behaving going through the pasture on our way to and back from school. Every year we attend a Christmas party at school which we help put up streamers and make bells to hang up and stars. We always got presents from school and at home within a week.

Church was always mandatory thing to do every Sunday. The minister would pick us up at the door every Sunday morning. Then we would either walk home or he would give us a ride back home. There was also a concert at our church every Christmas time and we got presents there also.

When I was about six years old, I went with my dad to go hunting and sure enough he got a jack rabbit. Dad said that I was big enough to carry the rabbit home, so dad put the back legs over my shoulder, and I started to walk back home. The rabbit was very long, I thought because it dragged in the snow front feet and head.

Then the next spring, one day, there was a team of horses coming up the back road west and south of the house. Then the horses stopped on the road and dad went to see what they wanted. They had a dog with them, and they were of course a pair of Indians. I guess they were mom and dad to someone. When dad talked to them, they wanted to trade the dog for a few chickens. The dog was a shiny black labrador, a very good water dog. One afternoon, my oldest brother and I went duck hunting, and my job was to hold the dog until my brother got done shooting the ducks.

When I released the dog, he brought the duck in from the pond. The dog would bring only one duck at a time into shore. We were very happy with the dog's work. Our dog was well fed, and we even built a house for him. The dog was never tied up at all. Always stayed at home and never followed us to school. We could run and play with the dog; he was very gentle with us kids and never got bitten.

Mom had two fly swatters, and I would ask mom if I could kill some flies, and she said I will give you one cent for every ten flies you killed. I told her that that was a good deal, so I made about five cents the first day. When I got paid, I asked if I could go to the store for candy and mom would say, yes you can. When I got to the store, I met my uncle and aunt for the first time. I asked aunty, what had happened to my uncle? and she told me that he had polio for a long time. My uncle was a very big man when I first met him. Then the next few times I was there, I learned that uncle could make violins, and he wrote a song or two and had them on records by someone else that sang his song that he wrote. They were not big hits at all.

Some of the weekends, mom would play the harp and sing a few songs which was entertainment for the family. Our dad and mom bought a lot of candy from uncle and auntie. In the summer times

I would find some pennies in the sand around the house which were spent on candy.

On fall I decided to chop wood for a night fire like splitting wood blocks. Then I had an accident that night and the axe head came off the handle and hit me on the head and broke the skin and made it bleed. My older brother took me in the in house and mom sewed me up with black thread. That night, I stayed in the new house so mom could keep an eye on me. About a week, mom took the stitches out.

Dumb things we used to do when we were young like my oldest brother bet my sister, he could walk on red hot coals, then I tripped on a plow and cut my knee, just a small cut. Mom put a towel and piece of cloth she tore up for bandits. Mom used a cream bought from Watkins dealer that travels around. I missed a few days of school because of the cold weather in the wintertime. I would walk away and get cold feet and return home.

My oldest brother would heat water in a five-gallon pail on the barrel stove we used in the homestead house. Then when it was hot enough, he would put in an old steel tub for us boys to bathe in. It took two or three pails to fill the tub up and had mom's homemade soap. The soap was also used as shampoo for the hair.

On weekends were our days for washing clothes which our old washing machine we used was the one grandpa and grandma used. Us boys would take turns to erank the washing machine. That was used in the spring, summer and fall only. In the wintertime the wash tub and the scrub board were used.

It was in the fall my oldest sister left the family when she was sixteen and went to the big city to stay at my aunt's place and attended university there. In university, she met and chatted with her future husband. They eventually got married and moved to Alaska, USA and had a family with him. Then shortly after my sister moved out then my mom had a girl then two years later, she had a son and that was the last of our family.

It was about eighteen months later that our family broke up and went in different directions. My older brother, younger brother, and sister and the baby and of course me all went with Mr. Jojo to a city. We did not know was there and stayed in a group home until we were adopted out to foster parents. We had to go to school and start a grade back because something to do with our school.

When we got to the group home, there was a big surprise to us, there was running water electricity and a television to watch and good meals. There were indoor washrooms, but I got used to cold out house before that. One of our workers took used to school by walking with us only three blocks away.

I like our group worker because she bought us stuff and took us out to see the city. Then one night she came and took us to the racetrack and told us her brother was driving one of the cars. That night I will never forget the group worker's brother got killed in the racetrack race. Right after the accident our group worker took us back to the group home and left right away back to the racetrack to see how her brother was doing. They took him to the hospital and there he died. The group worker took two weeks off to work.

It was a year and a half that we stayed in the group home and then was adopted out. My older brother and sister and the baby were taken to a farm about seventy-five miles from where my younger brother and I were taken to. My younger brother and I were also taken to a farm family.

That fall we went to school, and they set my brother and I back one grade to refresh our minds, I guess. I was not happy they set us back, it was a little disappointing. Although it was better at the new farm, my brother and I still missed our brothers, and sisters and mom and dad.

On the farm we had chores to do like cutting wood and helping in the barn and fill the water trough up for the cows and horses to drink out of. We also had to carry water in the house and make kindling for to start fire with.

One thing, my brother and I were happy to have lights in the house and barn and in yard light. There was also a T.V. in the living room. So, we could watch.

Our show on Saturday night was hockey night then on Sunday night was Don Messer and Ed Sullivan and of course Bonanza. The TV was only turned on weekends, but we had a radio to listen to in the mornings. Then the other thing was the outhouse and eations or sears catalogue used as toilet paper.

It was about two years after we were adopted when our foster mom passed away. Our foster mom had a tumor in her head and did not last that long and wanted to stay at home until she had to go into the hospital. After she passed away, our foster father's son-in-law and my brother and I and a neighbor help digged their grave and the ground was frozen hard, so we had to use a pick and shovel to get it to the standard depth.

Our foster father was a little hard on us boys until he got feeling better. It was the grieving process, I guess. Then shortly after that foster pa got a new job which paid only one hundred a month to look after the feedlot and cows and calves. In total of feeders were about four hundred and fifty heads. There were also about fifty heads of cows and calves that we took to pasture in the spring. When we moved the cows and put a calve on a wagon which one of us boys would keep the calf and cow would bawl for each other and the cow would follow the wagon which was pulled by a tractor. Then the rest of the herd would follow.

In the feedlot, there was a sick pen, and one also in the pasture loading area. The sick pens were used very little since the cattle would get such things as pink eye and foot rot or get bloated and had to stay on the sick pen for two or three days. Sometimes we got lucky and gave the bloat Eze in a pill form and had to crush up and put in a bottle and pour down the throat.

Then if that did not work there was a tube installed in the stomach between the second and third rib. Then also they had to watered by five-gallon pails in a cut in half drum as a watering bowl. One of our other chores was to make sure there were salt blocks in the wooden boxes and mineral bocks there also. The oilers had to be filled with oil for black flies and mosquitos.

The feeder cattle went in four different stages from mild chop to hotter chop in fatting process. Then when they got up to the right weight they were loaded for the market, and they were replaced by new ones.

When we loaded some cattle, we had to sort them out the day before they were shipped out. The trucks rolled in about four a.m. in the morning to load out. The reason for that was my brother and I had to go to school and foster pa need the help to load the cattle. Then when we got back home, we did a few chores then went off to school. I was glad it happens only once in a while because of short nights and long days.

It was about twice a month we would take our cream into the railway station which got loaded and sent to the big city to make cheese out of. Then when we were low on butter, we would turn our own with a butter maker. The butter maker was a big churn with paddles which had to be cranked.

The next thing was when the cream was separated the skim milk was needed to our calves and little bit to the pigs and to our potato peels were fed to the pigs mixed with grain that we had grind in an old wooden bin which was square. One of our tractors had a pulley which was used on the grinder machine for grain and in the process, it was very dusty and itchy. All the time we would be white as snow from the dust which happened at least once a month.

One year my foster pa took us in the fall to go trashing with one of our neighbors that still had a trashing machine. It was in the fall that we went threshing oats that he uses the binder to make sheafs out of. Anyway, when we started there were about four wagons with teams of horses to pull them. Then there were three men to a team of horse's wagon. There was stayed on the wagon and one of each side of the wagon pitching the sheafs up to the driver of the team of horses,

Then it was brought to the trashing machine and pitched in to remove the grain and the straw was blowen into a stack which was used as bedding for the livestock. The grain was put in a wagon and had to be shoveled onto a grain bin by hand. There was no grain augers used. From that time on we call that day our pioneer day because we got to learn how the pioneers harvest their grain.

That same summer and fall, my brother learned how to pick rock big and small ones on summer follow. Then the next chore was to help cut hay with three-point hitch tractor and mower and after it was dried from the sun it was rolled into windrows and then bunched into little stacks with a horse rake, which I sat on a seat and trip the rake when it was full of hay.

Then the hay was put on a hay rack wagon and hauled to the barn yard and stacked as a loose haystack. The oat sheaths are stacked in the yard next to the haystack. There were also straw bales brought into the yard for bedding for the animals.

There was a pair of Clydesdale horses which were used in the winter for hauling out the manure from the barn and hauled out to the garden and in the spring that was plowed in. The only problem was that when I went to feed the horses, they had an idea of squeezing me and foster pa said to use my elbow move the horses over so I could walk in between the horses.

The only vehicle our foster pa had was a nineteen forty-two dodge car. Which was used as a truck also. The car was used to haul all sorts of stuff like a calf and a ganie stack of pigs and bag of grain and chop. My brother and I took turns to hold the bag of piglets and help me hold down a calf that pa bought cheap from dairy farm.

One afternoon, our pa decided to go to town for mail and grocers and pa just about got into town when he was pulled over by a RCMP and the gas tank was tested and read purple fuel and pa got a ticket which was the sum of seven dollars. He said that one more dollar and he could have bought a drum of gas. Pa told the neighbor about the fine and being caught and the neighbor said that he would show pa how to change the color of purple gas to clear. They went to the garage and on the east side was six one gallon glass jugs of gas sitting in the sun. The sun bleached purple out of the gas.

On the farm, there were three tractors, one was a nine-n ford, the other was a D' John Deere and the third was a forty-four Massey Harris. Each tractor had its own job to do like the D' John Deere did the heavy work like plowing and one waying and picking rock especially the big rocks to pull out the ground with a chain. Then the Nine n Ford was used for the garden and haying and hauling a gas barrel to town and back. It was also used to haul cream cans to town and empty one back.

The Forty-four Massey Harris was used for discing and harrowing and seeding and on the binder to make oat shelves for the livestock. It was also used for hauling hay into the yard and hauling the oat shelves into the barn yard. Then the tractor was also used for the grain crasher since it had a belt pulley on the side. It was D' John Deere because of the brake on the John Deere.

The house was built years before the property was bought as the house was a log house. The log was standing straight up with a plaster in between the logs. Then eventually it was sheeted with plywood. The windows were single panes, and, in the winter, there was plastic installed on all the windows. The house had a cook stove and an oil heater in the living room. In the wintertime on cold days, when we woke up there would be ice on the water pail but was quickly thawed out once the fire was going in the cook stove.

In the summertime, when school was out, one of our jobs was to pick rocks and roots of the summer follow. The rocks were mostly limestone which was piled in a windrow. The roots were piled and burned in the wintertime. Then the job was to cut wood and pile it in the yard next to the yard light. If we got home late, we could cut wood up for the night.

One spring my brother and I and our classmates had a science project of planting tree which was spruce on the farm or in town where they lived. So, we planted the trees about four feet apart and used cow manure as fertilizer and had to water the tree regularly to start the tree to grow. We also picked weed and grass away from them, so the water was not a waste. Eventually they grow to be big trees.

Pa said they would not be cut down as long as he was alive which they were not. In the winter we had snow to shovel if we wanted to skate on the way out across the road from the house. My brother and I would invite our neighbors to come and skate with us after we shoveled the ice off. When we went skating our pa as we called him, he would go outside and put a tobacco can of oil rags outside and put of oily rags and start on fire to heat oil in oil pan so the car would start easily which took about an hour to heat up.

One year the owners of the feedlot brought a sixty-five Massey down for us to use for the feedlot which come in handy. We did not have to walk to the feedlot anymore. That was one and a half miles away from our farm. The tractor was also used for pulling dead steers that bloat or ate what we called iron stomach. It was also used to move bales around and to move bales in for bedding.

When I finished school at the end of June at the age of sixteen the bosses from the feedlot company also had a road construction company. They asked my pa if I could go to work on the road construction job they were doing.

When I worked on the road construction my job was to drive a tractor and a four sets of wabbles then went to a packer and back to the tractor and wabbles. Then about two weeks I was asked if I could drive a semi and water tanker since the guy quit and needed a driver for those units.

The water tank took about an hour to fill from dugout. The units had to be driven into the ditch to get close enough to get filled. The semi-truck was an older IHC truck with the muffler missing and the exhaust pipe was too short. Like it was half-way up the door, so you had to keep the window closed.

That fall, I drove a D 6 CAT for the company and used the CAT to bury rock piles and to cut back slope on steep sides. I learned how to run the CAT by keeping the blade in the ground and keeping moving those tracks all the time. Then I got to drive a D7 CAT and pulled a scraper to dig dugouts and was thinking how to run the CAT because it was cable control for the scraper.

It was in November, one of my friends asked me if I wanted to go to work. So, I phoned the company and went to the N.W.T. to work.

There were three of us from our hometown that went to work for that company. The job consisted of seismic work like bulldozing trees down on right of way for drillers to come and explore to see if they could find oil. Then once I had to plow snow off of a lake for the airplane to land with our grocers for camp. The cigarettes came in on our grocer's list by the cartoon and cost the same as back home that was one dollar a pack.

The next spring when the job was done. I went to the bigger town and got a stove and fridge brand new green in color for one thousand dollars. Then about five years later I sold out and moved and I got the same price as I bought everything for.

Then that summer I went back on road Construction. Went to different parts of the province to work with the same company. When I talked to my older sister that fall. I was told that my sister and her husband were going on a trail ride not too far from where they lived across the country. That was horses and wagons and a cuttle drive which was camping outside around bound fires. The trip took about two weeks to complete. They got permission from farmers to cross their land.

That fall I went to see my aunty and stayed with her for about a week then my first cousin came over and asked if I wanted to go to work. The next morning my cousin came over and we went shopping for stuff I needed to go to work with. Then my cousin picked me up and we left the next morning to a camp job that was building grain elevators and doing repair work on them. That winter I got laid off because we had to wait for the elevators to be emptied out. Then that winter I phoned my other cousin in Manitoba and got a job with him in the nickel mine. Then my brother and I went to our cousin's place to get ready to go to work. The first day was orientation and watching films and a tour of the mine facility parts. Then we were shown how to charge our lights for our hard hats. Then the next morning we went to work in the mine. After we got suited up in a wet suit and our hard hats on with the lights on, we went to elevator to take us down to the twenty-four hundred level.

Then when we got into the elevator, there was a boxed car that was repaired and had to be brought back down. The shaft with use to the railway tracks at the twenty-four hundred level. When we were going down the shaft, the eight foot opens like tunnels look like they were about a foot opens because we were traveling very fast because of the weight we were carrying. My brother and I worked there for about two months. Then decided that job was not for us to do. Then about a week my brother and I got a job doing hydro towers which we both liked because no wearing wet suits or had no more lights to look after. Then at Christmas time we went back home.

Then the next spring, I went back to working on the grain elevators and stayed with them for the next four years and went to a lot of different places in the province. Then in the spring of the fifth year I was laid off again and I went to a gravel crashing job in Alberta for a company. When I got to three jobs I started out as a laborer and worked my way up to operating the loader then to stack piling the crashed gravel with a D Eight CAT.

That year there were about two and a half million yards of graveled crushed. I eventually got to run the small crushed and look after changing the screens and getting a welder to build up the rollers that crushed the rocks. That job was pretty demanding like having to be there all the time. I stayed there until we were caught up.

Then when my job was done, I asked my older brother if he wanted to go to B.C. To work at a sawmill. Then we left for B.C. for the job and when we got there our job started at night shift. My older brother and I shared a motel room and slept all day and got up about six in the evening and had supper and got lunch made for the night shift.

One night on my shift, I was cleaning the log deck of limbs and stumps and small pieces of wood. Then I went to the tool shed and got a broom and I went sweeping. The next thing I knew I was laying down under the log deck amongst a bunch of tree parts. There were two guys who came to see if I was okay. The next morning, I woke up in the hospital which the nurse was giving me a needle for pain.

Apparently, I had passed out and my brother came to see me and told me what happened. I was walking along the log deck and there was a manhole left open and fell through the hole and hurt my back and neck on a stump that I was going to be move later that night. I was going to start the con very up to take the saw dust and limps and butts of the tree to the burner all our scraps were burned in a big burner.

I was in the hospital for about three weeks. I had three vertebral out of place, and they did not want to operate on me because of my spine being close to being pinch nerves off. I had a big scare, and I decided to go back home, and my older brother left a week before I got home or left the province. I was home for about two weeks and my younger brother told me he had a hard time finding work. I went to the doctors, and they said I could go back to work.

Then the next day, I looked in the newspaper that would be the western producer. There was a job for an operator for a six twenty-one buggy or scrapper in right terms. So, I phoned the company and got hired right away. That would of being on a Friday morning. The next thing I had to do was get a vehicle to get to work, so I went to the bank for a loan.

I got a loan and my car and plates and insurance. Then I needed tires on it and fuel to go to work. So, I ended it up as a five-hundred-dollar loan. The next Monday I had to be at work, so I left Sunday afternoon and stayed in the bunk house that was at the shop. By the way that would have been my second car. My first car was a nineteen fifty-three Chevrolet two door hand top which I paid fifty-five dollars. Anyway, I stayed with the company until freeze up. That winter I went back up north to work for the winter months. When I was on my days off from work up north my brother and I went skating and when we got there, I could smell gas from one of the cars. I checked it out and found out it was one friend that I bought my first car from. I told him and he went outside and fixed it.

Then the week later, I went back up north to work. I was surprised when I asked the stewardess how fast we were going to get airborne and she said about sixty miles an hour and then they turned the turbo on for more speed to raise the plane off the ground. It took about two hours to go to N.W.T. where I was going to work.

After we landed in the bigger town, we had to switch to a small plane to go to the camp. The foreman picks us up at the place we landed and took us to camp in a bombardier. Then we should us oar bunk beds and where the kitchen was where we ate. The next morning, we got up early, had breakfast and made lunch to go to work with. The camp consisted of about four trailers on runners. When was pulled by a D Seven CAT.

Then I got to run a D Six CAT on day shift. The CAT I was driving and all the rest of them had shoes on the blade so that the blade would not disturb the ground. The work consisted of clearing so many kilometers a day. Then night shift would go and pile the rest of the windrows and the D Seven would tramp the trees down so the wildlife could cross with very little effort.

One day, I had the job of making an air strip for the plane to come deliver our groceries. The ice was checked for thickness of at least thirty-six inches of ice needed to carry my CAT and the airplane. I made the runway about one hundred feet wide and two thousand feet long. It took most of the day to prepare the runway for the plane to land.

When the job was done up north for the winter I went home for a week. Then I went to visit my aunty and then went to the home stay while I was visiting friends, and the storekeeper asked if I heard about the car accident. I said no I did not hear about it then he told me. The accident happened on congraduation night. The young students were out having a party and when they were driving home across a bridge they met another car on the wrong side of the road.

There was three in one car and two in the other car and was head on collision which all five were killed. That summer I went back to work on the grain elevator. In the winter came and was very cold and there was another accident that killed two people I knew. The accident happened when some friends of mine were coming home from work. That night there was a blizzard, and it was very poor visibility when the head on collision happened.

The young man was working in the shop repairing heavy equipment and I supposed had a beer or two before leaving the town. Since there was no bar in our hometown. The three of them hit something and all were killed. One of them was found about a hundred and fifty feet in a field. The person was rejected from the car on impacted.

The next couple of years I was on the road construction when I had may accident one weekend I was coming home and I made it home and had a coffee with my foster pa. My foster pa told me to stay and have a sleep and I could pick up my brother in the morning but being bull headed like I was I said no I could pick him up and my friend want to go home also. My foster pa asked how many hours we work that week. I was very tired not at all we were drinking only coffee and pop. Anyway, we left my foster pa and was going the back road to go to town, and I did not get very far when we both fell asleep while I was still driving my car. When I hit the dead-end road and also there were no signs to say a dead-end road ahead. Anyway, I totaled the car off and went to a friend's place for help. The friend took me and the friend to the hospital and his wife phoned my foster sister to let foster pa know about the accident.

I was in the hospital for about three days and that night my roommate died about two a.m... I was scared because that was the first time I was close to a dead person. My friend got about five stitches and went home. I was not that lucky, I got twenty-one stitches and had to stay in the hospital. I had to drink fluids through a straw and tomato soup through a straw for the first few days.

In about a week I was released from the hospital and got a surprise when I got home. My foster pa brought me a car at the auction mart and had it check out for safety wise. He paid about two hundred for the car at the auction mart. The car was not as new as the one I smashed up. But small so it was cheap on fuel what I was looking for. The car I had was nice and small and easy to drive and I missed that car. But that's what happened in an accident which consisted of a steering wheel bent down past the signal light arm switch. Also, the windshield was all smashed and from end damage then within two weeks I was ready to go back to work. When I had my accident there were no police involved at all. There also was no insurance claim at all.

One winter day when I was working in the N.W.T. my brother went to town and went skating. Then that night was a hockey game which my brother had to play in. After the hockey game the caretaker said to my brother that he heard that his brother had passed away. So, my brother asked him who told him that and my brother was worried. My brother thought I was killed up north at work and was not told about it.

I was a heavy-duty drinker when I was not working, and they thought I got drunk and got into antifreeze. That is how they thought I had killed myself with the poison in the antifreeze. Only thing I know that the antifreeze was poison. My brother told me when I got home from work when we went curling in a bonspiel which I played third place. My brother and foster pa were very happy to see that I was okay.

In our small farm community in town there were about fifteen people that lived there. We were about one and half miles from town's people were retired farmers and the school teachers were farmers' wives that got their degree for teaching. My brother and I went to school from grade two and grade three until the highest we could go in the school was grade eight which I completed. In the summertime in our school break we went swimming at the lake which we were based there and back each day. The swimming lessons lasted about two weeks each year.

One fall I went to the city to see one of my aunties on my dad's side of the family. I was visiting and she was telling me stories about the early days of her life which were very interesting. She told me about her sons, what they were like growing up and what they became. One of them was a construction worker and the other son was a building engineer for a grain company.

The son that worked on construction was married to a native lady and had three children with his wife, which my auntie told me that if he got her pregnant you marry her. That's what happened that you got married in the old days when you did a bad thing. Like you got married then started a family. Anyway, on the weekend my first cousin came over and we and a few beers in the basement. Then my first cousin went downtown to one of his friends first cousin went downtown to one of his friends and got a quart of moonshine which was about ninety proof which he should me by burning the alcohol on a spoon which burn blue. I had about half a glass and passed out. It was too strong for me even with mix. The next week my friend and my first cousin left to go to Winnipeg. When we arrived in Winnipeg my first cousin stayed there, and my friend and I went onto thunder bay for a week. Then we came back to Saskatchewan.

I stayed in the city for a week with my aunt and then I got a phone call for a week on road construction for the rest of the summer. Then I ended up back at home for the winter working for farmers. The farmers would go out on the pipeline for the winter months.

The next spring I went to my auntie's place and was only there for a week and my first cousin asked if I wanted a job on the grain elevators. I was getting paid $10.00 per hh in the mid-seventies. I worked for about three months then I bought a new car. The new car was only fifty-two hundred dollars to buy. I stayed with the grain company for a few years.

Within about three years my brother had a small acre age with a house on it. Anyway, I got permission from my brother to dig a well on the property. When I got permission, I asked my foster pa if he could help me dig a well. The next week I had offered him work.

When I was working I brough back a bunch of two by six planks and a lot of two by fours to build a garage on the place also. So, when we started digging the well, I had borrowed a well machine that was used by a horse drawn machine. The machine worked very well. The first days were getting used to the machine and how it worked. I have bought a D John Deere for the job.

When I had to go down the well my pa cranked me down on a cable and I sat on a chair with a crowbar on my lap. The reason I went down the well was to remove the rocks from the side walls which the auger was hitting and would hold the auger up from touching the bottom of the well. My pa lowered a pail down after I got off the chair so I could put the rock in the pail and was brought up to the top and pa emptied and I got down to about thirty-three feet when I hit a big rock. The next morning, I had fifteen feet of water in the bottom of the well.

When my pa came over to see what I was doing and told him how much water was in the well. Then we had coffee, and my pa said it is time to build a crib for the well. Anyway, he had told me what to get in the meantime what I would need to build. Then we built the cribs which were only sixteen feet long and which took two sections. After they were built, we used the well machine to lower them into place. I had bought a cement culvert to set on top of the wooden crib.

Then there was a lid made out of a plywood to keep the water clean. The next year I fixed up the house with new curtain and wall panels and new curtains.

That fall I got married to a lady that was not far from where I lived. They were a poor family, and I loved the lady I married. I was with her for about a month and then went to work up north again.

When I got home for Christmas break, we had a great Christmas with her family at our place. That Christmas my wife made a perfect turkey dinner which was enjoyed by everyone. My wife was eleven years younger than me, but we loved each other. We had lots to eat all the time that we were together and when I was working.

The next spring my wife got pregnant, and I was a very happy person. I was going to be a father which was going to make me to be happy and proud father. It was about two to three months in her pregnancy that she started to miscarriage. Her father was at his place when my wife and I got to the house, and I told her dad what was happening, and he said we would take his car to the hospital. The wife got checked in and was told that we had to take her to another hospital twenty-five miles away to see a specialist.

When we got there, they had to do a D+C to her and they said they could not save the child she was carrying. They did more than a D+C to her which they tied her cord so she could not get pregnant again. It took me twenty-two years to find out about her tubes being tied. I asked her dad why they did that, and he said he found out the doctors thought she was mentally handicapped.

That was not the case at all. My wife's dad told me when I was dating her what had happened when she was born. She had problems with her eyes and her dad took her to city hospital for and eye operation when she was twelve years old. The doctors removed her eyeballs and tied the knot in the cords to straighten her eyes. The eye job was not perfectly done. You could notice it was a poor job done.

The next spring, we moved to a small town where my mother lived. My wife and her dad and brothers and her sisters moved with us. Then my brother-in-law came to live with us. And his wife and kids. My brother-in-law had an Irish setter dog about one and half years old. The dog had epilepsy which he was taking medicine for. By the time he was about two years old he had about nine to twelve epilepsy fits a day.

Then I took the dog to the vet, and he said he would put him down because he could do nothing for the dog. I said O.K. and within an hour the dog had died. Then I took the dog and buried him. When we moved into the house the rent was seven hundred a month plus utilities. About two weeks my wife dad and I went to work for a grain company repairing elevators in different province. It was south in the city.

My father-in-law and I were the only two working on the job doing repairs and building a new catwalk and fix six bins bottoms shots and in bottoms. The job I hated tinning the bin bottoms of the elevator. Another job was to clean weigh scales and adjust the weights.

Then the next job was in home province. It coincided with lifting an elevator and taking out old crib and installing new cement floor and new crib and timbers. Shortly after that job was done my mother passed away on December 26th, the day after Christmas. My mom was waiting for her first pension cheque. But the time was not right for her since she was only sixty-four and would have turned sixty-five in six weeks.

Then I had a job working on a screening converter to load truck with gravel for number one highway just out of the city that was about six months after mom passed away. Then I was at work when a police officer came to me and asked If I could come to the office after work. So, I did, and he asked if I could identify my stepfather's belongings.

When I looked and said that was his stuff, I asked what had happened? The RCMP Officer said that my stepbrother was killed this morning on long side of number one highway where he was picking bottles. Another older gentleman was coming from a city and heading to Calgary to see a nephew. Then the older gentleman had a heart attack and lost control of the car he was driving. My stepfather, his name was Joe, had an epilepsy fit and was lying on the ground at the bottom of the ditch. At that time the older gentleman hit the ditch and drove Joe. That is why the only thing was proper way to identify my stepfather. Since his face was smashed up pretty bad and the RCMP Officer would not let me see him. The older gentleman was taken to city hospital and survived. The daughter of the older gentleman was told he was not supposed to drive at all.

It was about a week later we had a funeral for Joe and then the house was sold. Then it was not too long after that I moved to Alberta to work on the grain elevator again. The one in a city was the last one I helped build. Then shortly after that I got divorced from my wife. My wife wanted to stay in Saskatchewan, and I want to stay in Alberta to start a new life, but she wanted to stay close to her family which she grew up with.

It was mostly my fault we got a divorce because I wanted a family of my own and my wife could not have any more children. Which I found out later after my ex-wife passed on. That when she had the miscarriage the doctors tied her cords so she could not have any more children. The reason they tied her cords because she was young, she had problems with her eyes and her dad took her to the hospital an eye specialist to straighten her eyes out. So, they had to tie some cord in the back of her eye to straighten them out. So, when my wife had miscarriage, the doctors thought there was a mental problem and took it on themselves to tie her cords. So, she could not get pregnant again. They never let her father know. If we had stayed together, we would have had twenty years before she passed away.

Anyway, my wife and I had a good time together. I bought a ¾ ton truck and a camper and she come to work with me one summer. Then the next summer we had our honeymoon by going to Montana USA. With another couple that were friends of ours. When we got there, we got a motel room for a week and went shopping, played pool and went to the show in the town theater. Then we headed back home and made it safely, everyone was happy.

This happened on a Sunday night when I was going to work in Saskatchewan. A car just passed me, and I noticed a bunch of sparks coming from the back end of the car. I got ahead of them and put my four-way flasher on, and they stopped to see if everything was okay. When he came to the car, I was driving I told him there were sparks flying out the back end of his car.

He told me it was the muffler and tail pipe dragging on the highway and he would tie it up again. He thanked me and I left for work.

That fall I was driving heavy equipment. The company was bringing the machines home for repairs and new tires. I was following behind and was the last unit. I was trying to keep up and going and we were really going to shop. I tried to get back to normal speed by hitting the brake pedal with my foot which did not help. So, I kicked the fuel pedal and then it went back to normal speed.

When we got to the shop, I told the mechanic about what happened. Then the next morning we went in a bus to another job site to bring some more units to the shop. When we got there one unit had a flat tire and one other had a back transmission problem. The mechanic disconnected the drive shaft u joint, and I used the front motor. By the way the were all twin motor units. Then all of us drivers got the units back to the shop for repair work to be done in the winter months. They were ready for spring work again.

That fall I went to work in the N.W.T. but I had to fly out of Edmonton to Inuvik then a small plane to camp. Then at the same time my stepfather was a firefighter in Edmonton at that time. Then there was a firefighter exchange program with Australia and my half-brother was stationed in Pert for the winter months. My sister went to Australia for Christmas or past before or after to see my brother in Pert. Then they went to Sydney Australia for the weekend.

When my brother got back from Pert Australia, he said there were more grass fires then house fires. So, it was like a vacation which was a paying experience which was good for him and his wife. The program only lasted about six months. It was about five years later when he retired and moved away from the city.

One thing I can tell you is that in life there is a mystery thing that happened for a good reason like my oldest half-brother and his wife had a set of twins. Then twenty-five years later my brother that was last born and his wife had a set of twins on the same day and same month. It is very seldom that ever happens to one family. Anyway, one of them had a set of twins as a boy and a girl the other had a set of twins as two boys. I had the privilege to meet the boy and girl only so far. We have a strong out family as you can tell. We talked about every ten or so years apart we are close but not close.

When my dad and mom got married in British Columbia. That was in nineteen fifty-two and a year later I was born. Then we moved to the homestead. Then I was named after grandpa. Then my other brothers and sister were named after my dad's brothers and sisters. But dad only had one baby girl before we split up.

So far, in my life, I have met of dad's family two brothers and four sisters that I can remember. Then on mom's side I met on brother. There was a big family but did not get to meet many relatives at all. I did not get a chance to meet my grandparents at all. They all had passed away when I was very young at age. Anyway, my mom's family owned an orchard in B.C., and I was told my dad was a coal miner in B.C. also. It must have been at a bar or friends or relative that they met.

Anyway, my relatives had all kinds of trades to work at. From mining to orchards to bus driving to farming and into music so I was told. There was one uncle that made fiddles and bows when he retired and had written a song or two and had on records which I had them but lost them also. Like everything else I like was always lost out of my life. I have no pictures or anything that was handed down to me.

One summer day, I was hitching hiking back home when about three girls were driving a car. They pulled over and asked me where I was going home for the weekend. Then I said no I had to get home to help my old man with chores. That's when I did a lot of hitch hiking since I couldn't afford a car at that time. I was only making about sixty dollars a week. Then when I got laid off for winter UIC paid me seven dollars a week which equals twenty-eight a month.

Lots of hard work for little money we got. Just the going rate, same as farmers paid very little because of the ceremony thing and the government also milk, eggs, meat and cream.

One thing that never happened was going to church. Ever since my brother and I were adopted. Before we were adopted, we always went to church on Sundays. The church was a Baptist and located in the country. The minister would always come to our place and pick us up for church and after service he would bring us home. All of us kids could hardly wait to go to church because it was something special for us to lean about the bible and Jesus Christ. My brothers and my sister had the best record for attending church then our whole school.

After we got adopted out to a farm family things changed a lot in our life. There were no more going to church on Sunday's. Also, we missed playing outside with our brothers and sister. There was no more walking to school and playing on the way like all boys and girls do. Then there were no summer holidays in which we always went to the pines for a picnic and picked blue berries, also raspberries and currants.

Since we were young the summertime was long and full of fun like going hunting with my older brother. Then also robbing eggs from duck's nests. Then there was making money from mom like killing flies for a penny each one. That merited ten flies bought ten cents worth of candy. Then there were always chores to do like getting wood for winter. Then there was cleaning chicken cage out and putting new straw in for them.

There was always something to do like help wash clothes with a crank style washing machine. Then also weed the garden and help clean the well out of which was thicky because of the sandy bottom walls. Then we went to use the York maple leaf truck; we had to crank it to start it up. The truck had poor tires and a glass battery to use for the lights.

Mom would try and wash clothes at least once a week. There were a lot of dirty diapers to clean and dry on a clothesline. When we lived on the homestead, we were a long way from any hospital. Anyway, mom was our doctor and nurse and babysitter and cook. She was a very busy lady being in that parent role.

It also seems to be in our family that a two year apart happen right from the beginning. Most of us kids were born on the homestead. There was a nanny called in to help with the deliverers. The reason for that was we lived too far from a hospital, little alone, a town of any size. My dad would say to us kids go play and do not come in the house until I say it was okay to do so.

In grandpa's house where my brothers and I lived. In the old house there were only cardboard boxes on the walls which thin car lids to hold the cardboard on. There was a forty-five-gallon drum laid on its side with a door and chimney used as a stove. Only wood was burned which was cut up in the fall. My oldest stepbrother and dad used an old ten twenty IHC tractor and old buss saw to cut the wood into blocks for the kitchen stove and the barrel heater.

In the old house there were single army style beds which were big enough to hold two small boys. On the beds there was no mattress but there were clothes spread on the springs. Then there was an army styled blankets to cover up with. Our oldest stepbrother kept the fires going all night. Then he had to make sure the fire did not get too hot, which would set the house on fire.

One summer, I went to work out for a crushing company they out me as a car operator to stockpile the gravel away from the crusher. In a couple of months, the crusher operator trained me how to run the crusher. I had learned how to change screens and when to call a welder in to build up drums.

When I was working in that town, I asked my mom to come down for a weekend since she was in Alberta before. The next day after mom arrived, we went to the museum then to a swinging bridge and to a coal mine shaft like dad worked on in B.C. Then the next day we went to see the hoodoos and the dinosaurs' bones. The third day mom went home, and I went back to work in the crusher. I end up crashing about a million cube yards of graves in that town.

That fall I spent time with my mom and her husband. Things we done were going fishing trips was one of mom's favorite things to do. When mom caught a fish, she would get so excited and got the fish and she would ask me to unhook the fish. Then she would rebait the hook and try for another one. The other thing she liked doing was canning the fish and cleaning them up. There were many things mom and her husband liked doing including picking bottles out of the ditch for extra cash.

Then about four years later my mom passed away. What had happened my mom had a breast removed years before because of cancer. Then one day it came back and ended her life. Then six months later my mom's husband and also my stepfather was in an accident that took his life.

When I got back to town the RCMP asked if I could identify the bag, he was carrying the morning he left to pick bottles. The RCMP told me that my stepfather was too messed up to be identified in person by looking at the body. Then a few days later the funeral was arranged and took place in the town my mom and stepfather had retired in. It was a small town along the number one highway.

When the accident happened, the older men had a heart attack and went and went off the highway. At that time my stepfather had an epilepsy attack. Until today, I still think he forgot to take his morning pills for his condition. My stepfather was out that morning like always picking bottles and pop cans to generate a little more income for himself. Anyway, what happened to my stepfather was in the ditch picking up bottles and cans. When the older gentleman had a heart attack and lost control of the car.

My mom passed away on boxing day and a few years later my father passed away. What was meant to be my folks were buried in the same cemetery side by side. They were only twenty years apart. They got along very well and enjoyed each other's company. They always went shopping together and traveled together.

My baby brother was born at home when dad was at a good age of seventy-two years old. Mom would have been fifty-two then. That was the last child to be in our family. It works out that there was two years apart from the oldest to the youngest. Some people thought that it was strange to be that precise. I think it had a big part of what God had in plan for us.

Between the homestead life and the adopted life, it was a hard way to live. Then also it was comfortable way to live, and it was a learning experiment. Every day there was something to learn and know what the right and wrong way was of doing things. Both of my father was hard of us, which was good learning lesson.

My uncle on my mom's side was eighty-four years old when he first got married. The wedding was very big, so I was told by my oldest brother. And the lady was eighty-two years old. So, I made a joke about uncle that he got tired of canning his sock and could not see so well. That's why he got married. Shortly after the wedding I got word that my first cousin's wife on my dad's brother's son had passed away. Then I was invited to go to the funeral which I knew the family very well, Because I lived with the family with my brother in Manitoba.

About ten years or so earlier my first moved from Manitoba to Alberta where the run of taxi busses for a few years. Then my cousin worked in a warehouse for a few years. My first cousin daughter graduated and worked for a lawyer firm. Then my first cousin's son graduated and went to Vancouver and enlisted in the NAVY which he stayed until he retired.

When my first cousin and family went camping one summer before they moved, I mean years before they thought of moving to Alberta. There was an accident that happened that killed his son. What happened was that they were at the lake for a weekend trip. My first cousin bought new inflatable swimming toys. The one his son used had malfunctioned when he was out of the lake. He drowned and had no backup safety jackets on.

When my brother and a friend of ours and me worked on grain elevators. The three of us worked on scaffold as a crew. When we got about halfway up, we would slide the ropes down for coffee breaks and lunch breaks. At night we were told to bring the scaffold down to reload with siding and paint nails. There was a special way of sliding down the rope of using your feet as brakes.

When I was working on the grain elevators repair crew I bought a Skidoo toboggan. I used it on weekends when I was off work. One weekend I was staying with a farmer, and I took the Skidoo out to my foster father's place and stayed for supper. Then after supper and a smoke and talk for about two hours left.

That night that I had supper with my stepfather, foster pa had left to go to the farm I was staying at. It was snowing when I jumped on the snow toboggan to go to the farm with very poor visibility to be out of the snow mobile. I got lost in the snowstorm and blowing wind and I was going across the country and open fields.

When the accident happened, I had hit a fence wire, and the wire broke and cracked my windshield on the snow mobile. I was pretty lucky that I had ducked down behind the windshield when I hit the three strands of barbwire. Then it took me about two hours to get to the farm, so it was about midnight when I got there.

A few years later I bought a motorcycle, and it was a nineteen fifty-three. The same year I was born. It was a three hundred CC street bike which I paid four hundred dollars for it. The first time I rode the bike on the road home on the back roads. It was about halfway home when I hit a sandy patch and upset the bike. That was the first time I drove a motor bike, and it was very heavy to lift back on its wheels. When I get it back on the solid ground, I make it go pretty fast where I should steer it and hold it upright. Then had to learn how to balance myself on the bike.

When I was about ten years old, and my brother was about eight years old when our foster father bought us each a CCM bicycle to ride around the farm and to our neighbors. Then once we could ride it properly, we could go to town on the weekend only for about two hours. Then I would make tea and put it into a quart jar and wrap it with newspaper and an elastic band to keep the tea warm and made two baloney sandwiches and took them to the field my foster pa was cutting for hay.

Then that fall after the hay and oat shelves were all in the yard and the grain was in the bin and the chop was made. When it was cold enough to freeze our neighbors dug out and the ice was thick, we were allowed to go skating. Our new skates were bought when the harvest was done. Then we also got our neighbors' boys to come and skate with us. The next winter my brother and I were signed up to play hockey in the minor league. I was not good on my skates because of not enough practice on them and I had weak ankles also. I had planned to play hockey as a goalkeeper and my brother played light wing and sometimes left wing for our schools' hockey team. Sometimes I was spare but was just important as the players on the team. If someone got hurt, I took his place. We also skated in our own kink in town.

When my brother and I were young and until we were in our teens the farm was a very busy place to be at. When it became late summer into fall that was the busiest time of the year. There was hay to be cut and dried enough that we could use the horse rake to bundle it up. It made it easier to load on the hay wagon which our foster pa built the rack. Then it was harvesting time which we used an old horse drown binder to make sheaves for the cattle and horses.

The crops were mostly oats and barley sometimes mixed for feed grain in sheaves. The hay was always put up loose in a stack no bales only sometimes we got straw bales for bedding in the barn.

Then we were to cut our hay stacks a cutter was used. It looks like a scale blade, only shorts with three or four blades and a piece to put your foot down on and it would out the hay up. The hay was always nice and green color inside.

The horses were big Clydesdale horses and were put in the barn in the wintertime and got fed an oat shelf once a day and the rest of the time just hay. The cow's milk would get tobacco can of chop when it was milking time in the morning and just before our supper time. Then after each milking the milk was poured into a cream separator and put in a refrigerator to keep cool until there was enough to put in cream cans and ship off by train to cheese factory.

Our foster parents have three tractors, and the smallest one was used the most. The smallest tractor was a nine N ford with a three-point hitch was good for use in the garden and also used for haying. Then it was used for taking cream to town to the railway station and tagged. I was very surprised how well our foster mom could handle the tractor.

Then the bigger tractor was used for patting in the crops and breaking new land with a plow. Then use a one-way disk to break it up to be planted. But first, the roots and stamps and stones had to be picked and then in the wither the roots and stamps we barned.

My brother and I grew up in a small community, maybe about 100 people in town with the surrounding farms. In town there were two grocers' stores and gas station and a school, a post office and a municipality office and a train station. There once was a hotel which burned down a few years before we got to the foster home. One summer we went to the dump and shot as many rats with a twenty two with two boxes of twenty two shells. My brother and our friend and I took turns shooting the varmints. One of our friends had a shot gun. We would never kill all the rats because they would hide on us.

Our foster pa had one brother that lived in engaged and one sister not for sure where she was located. Then our foster mom's side of the family was her daughter and brother that lived in southern Saskatchewan and her mom that lived in the same town as the farm was located. In the wintertime I would bring in the wood and coal into the house for our foster mom's mom. We called her grandmother, and she would make tea and always had cookies for me. Then she would give me two dollars for bringing in coal and wood and pail of water.

Our foster pa bought his mother-in-law's homestead quarter of land. Pa ended up with three quarters of the land. Which one was very stoney and was all bush that was used as a pasture, and one was used for growing crop, and one was used for hay that was wild brome and alfalfa and timothy grass. That one that had a lot of stones was a lot of limestone which are flat and easy to break up. There were some big ones; we used a stone boat and longer chain to pull off the field.

I do remember that there was a long row of rock on one side of the field. Every time we would dig or cultivate or harrow it would bring up more rock to be picked and hauled off the field. Sometimes it would be a big one and we had to use a shovel and a crowbar to pry them out or put a chain around to get pulled out. I like the small ones which are easy to pick up. The reason for picking rocks is that they would not break the machinery, and it is easy to arrow crops.

After a few years of road construction work I decided to try my hand at crushing gravel. I had helped crash and stockpile about ten million cubic yards at different places. Then when work got slow my older stepbrother and I went to B.C., to work in a sawmill. Both of us worked the night shift from midnight plus eight in the morning. About two in the morning when I was sweeping the log deck off bark, small pieces of branches. That night the electrician did not put the cover over a hole he was working in.

Of course, the electrician works through the day shift. That was when the accident happened. I fell in the open hole and landed on some stumps and pieces of logs and branches on my back and hit my head. I crawled out and went to the office. Then the ambulance was called, and I went to the hospital for two weeks on my back needles for pain in my back. I had dislocated three vertebrae up between my shoulders and neck and I got the needle in my rump.

After I got out of the hospital I went back to work, and my stepbrother went back home. Then about a month later I was offered a foreman job for the company. Then I turned it down because I was by myself and had no friends. Then I took off home but only stayed there for a week and found another job in the western producer newspaper. It was a job that I had experience in.

When also got home my brother told me that he could not find a job. I told him it was easy, so I phoned and got a job for Monday morning working on road construction operating a motor scraper. Before I start the job, I need a vehicle to get there with. The next day my foster pa and brother and I went to town to buy a car and plates and insurance. But first I had to go to the bank to get a loan for the car and plates plus insurance and enough for fuels and tires plus battery. My whole bill came to five hundred dollars. I still had two hundred left.

That fall I bought a house in town for the sum of one hundred and twenty-five dollars from a farmer. Then when I got laid off for the season, I draw UIC which paid me a big seven dollars a week. That UIC paid for my fuel for the store and power and a few groceries. Our foster pa helped with meat and potatoes and vegies from the farm. Which was a big help.

The next few years I stayed on road construction. The job took me to a lot of different places. I worked as an operator in labor jobs like fencing and installing steel and cement culverts. The cement culverts were very hard to roll into place and connect together. There was the job of nestaking the road for elevation. Some places had to be cut down and other places had to be built up. Then there was the job of cutting back slope of the ditches. You had to learn really quick to keep your blade in the ground unit on level ground.

When the road construction was done then I decided to go back to doing grain elevator repairs. Then also help build a few new ones. Then there also was the job of tearing down the old elevators that my uncle had helped build in his earlier years. One place we tore down seven elevators four annex's and two bull pens. There was a lot of work getting the elevator ready to be torn down. Like taking the grain belt out and cups off the belt. Then lowering the motor and taking the spouts off and also the conveyer belt to disconnect and removed. Then the cupil to be pulled off the elevator.

It was late fall on a weekend that I was going to Prince Albert Saskatchewan to see my uncle and auntie. Thet morning was nice and clear when I left home. Then the closer I got to Prince Albert Saskatchewan it became foggy so bad at time you could not see the yellow line or white line on the highway. The fog was only in low yayn places.

My uncle and auntie had bought a house in Prince Albert Saskatchewan where they had retired. The both of them worked as switchboard operators for SaskTel. I stayed for dinner, and we talked about the hardships they had in life and the old days. Also, the trip they made from the USA to Canada. Then also about her brothers and sisters and how they got along.

When I was in Prince Albert at my aunties place, she told me where my father was. My father was in a hospital in the auxiliary ward. When I went to visit, dad did not know who I was at all. But I think in back of his mind he knew I was one of his kids. Dada properly thought later I was the one who went hunting with him and carried the jack rabbit home. When dad thought about something he would rub his chin like I kind of remember you.

Mom had known us kids until she passed away. The reason for that is she only had cancer and a good solid mind. We did not talk about the life we had on the homestead at all. We mostly talked about the ranch her and stepdad had worked on. When mom passed away on boxing day that is the one day that I feel sad about losing my mother each year.

Before this happened to mom, I had been in a hospital over an accident I had. The one night I had an experience I will never forget. An older person was next to me, I mean I was in the same room I was in, and he passed away. Any way the nurses were calling his name for it seemed like half an hour. Then the nurse calls out "code blue code blue!" a few times. Then he unhooked his intravenous and took him down the hallway. Then one nurse came back into my room and said everything was going to be okay. That was the second time I had seen a dead body in my presents. I had at that time was scared that was going to happen to me. From then on, I did things safer wise, and a lesson well learned.

There was one day around Christmas time I phoned my stepsister in Florida and was talking. When I was talking to her, she said that she missed the snow and cold winters in Canada. Another thing my sister wanted was for me to come and her husband. One Christmas when I phoned her it was seventy Degrees Celsius and lots of snow. I never got to spend any Christmas another time with her. But it would of nice to meet her two sons and daughter.

There was a family reunion in Edmonton Alberta. The reunion took place at my stepbrother's place, and everyone made it except my younger brother. That was a short reunion because I had to go to work the same as my young sister. Then at least I got to meet my brother-in-0law and see my sister for the first time in a long time since she moved away from the homestead. My oldest stepsister looked a lot like my mom. But if I had met or seen them, I would not recognize them all.

Then my c/w wife and I headed out to where we lived after we had a barbeque steak and a few beers. We left about seven p.m. and got home five hours later. I was very tired after driving ten hours that day. Then I had to leave for work Sunday afternoon to go to camp job. When I was driving a tempo car it was easy on seal and did not burn no oil.

When it comes to the family, my oldest stepsister moved when I was very young from my grandparent grandma's homestead. My stepsister was about sixteen when she went to live with our auntie in Regina Saskatchewan. I was too young to remember her at all. I do remember my older brother and sister talking about her. Anyway, when we were at the reunion my sister told me that when she left the homestead. Then she went to Regina then to Alaska where she got married. Then my sister and her husband had two boys and a daughter.

After years of marriage, my sister and her husband got a divorce. Then she moved to the Southern USA, which was Florida with her children. Then met her new husband who worked on construction jobs. Then one fall when I phoned her, and she said her husband was working in Philadelphia USA. Then when her husband came home for a weekend and a doctor's appointment. The morning, he had his doctor appointment he had a heart attack at the doctor's office. Then they took him to the hospital and had bypass heart surgery. He came out of the hospital. A few years later, my oldest sister passed away from bone cancer. Where her daughter still lives in the same city. When I phoned my sister in Florida, she said that they had survived three hurricanes and hailstorm and strong winds.

One reason my stepsister wanted me to come to Florida so I could go to Disney land and see the Grand Canyon. And then off to yellow stone parks and have a day at the car racing track. Then there was the orange and fruit orchards that grow in Florida and the surrounding area.

Getting back when I was working on the grain elevators in a small town in Saskatchewan. I had bought a new car a few months before I had to get a repair job done on the car. I took the car to a dueler shop to get it repaired. I stayed in the camp until my car was fixed on Saturday night when the parts came in. Anyway, it was Friday night I went for supper at the bar restaurant. Then I went to a bar for a few drinks when I met this girl. Then her and I played pool and had a few drinks and talked about work and where she was from. Then later that night she came over to the trailer I was staying in after the night.

Then about a month later I saw her and her brothers that came to talk to me. Then she told me that she was pregnant and told me that I was not supposed to try and see the girl or her family. I never saw her again or her family of my child that was to be born next summer. I wish things would have been different at that time of my life. Her family had a mixed farm and pretty big. Then two years later I met my wife to be and that fall in November we decided to get married. The falling spring my wife got pregnant which made us very happy and hoping for a son or daughter which every way was blessed with. Then about six weeks later into her pregnancy she miscarriage which her dad and I took her to the hospital for about five days and I stayed close by all the time she was in.

When my wife was in the hospital when she had her miscarriage, they did a D+C on her and tied her cords. Then years later I was told that the doctor in them years were doing experimental test on young woman for some reason or other. Then also it was years later after she passed away that I went to see her father. When I went to see her father and her brother that he had mentioned to me that her cords were tied. The reason was the doctor thought was my wife was unstable with mental problems. Which was not true, and she had an operation on her eyes when she was young.

About a year and half after my wife got out of the hospital we moved out of our small town from Northern Saskatchewan. Then we ended up in Southern Saskatchewan where mom was living in a nether small town. Within four months we invited my wife's father and his sons and daughter to our place in a small town. Within two months of moving to small town my father-in-law went to work with me on the grain elevators. Our first job was

South of Winnipeg, Manitoba. That is when we stayed at a camp to do a repair job. We had to tear out an old plate form at the top of the crib. We used four by six timbers and flooring was two by six with three quarter inches spacing. Then we had to tin bin bottoms and chang spouts. Then we cleaned the pit and then we changed the cups on the conveyor belt and called the legs. Then the conveyor belt had paddles to be changed, and a new linen installed. Which took about six weeks to complete.

The wife and I tried for five years to have a child. We could not figure out why my wife was unable to get pregnant. In the between time my wife and I bought a truck and a small trailer. When I was working on road construction my wife stayed in the trailer and cleaned and cooked meals for us at breakfast and supper time. At weekends we would go out for dinner and tour the countryside. A year after we got married, we decided to go on a honeymoon to the United States with another couple about our age. That was good to spend time together.

My wife and I would have known that my wife could not have any children. Then we would adopt a boy and a girl, which would have been good company for my wife when I was at work. That would have given a stronger bond between us since we both wanted to have children. Then also I would have stayed with her until her passing away.

After about a year from the divorce my ex-wife got re0married. The person she lived with had bought a small farm not far from her dad's place. I was told she grew a big garden and did a lot of canning. Each year until her passing with her big garden stuff. My ex-wife's father said I was mistaken to get a divorce in the first place. Her new husband was fourteen years older than her and treated her poorly, so what I was told.

When my ex-wife was laying on her death bed her husband was going out with one of the nurses in the hospital. Then when he was supposed to visit his wife, he was dating a nurse. My ex-wife passed away in January of the year of two thousand at the age of thirty-seven years old.my ex-wife passed away with leukemia cancer and suffered for quite a long time. If I was still married to her, I would have stayed at her side until the end. I still miss her lots of time when I think back of the good times that we had shared.

Then about a year before I got married, I had lots of bad nightmares. Each night I had dreamed that I was falling and hitting the bottom of something. When I hit the bottom, I would wake up in bed with a sweaty forehead and back. When I talked to some of my friends, they told me that my bad dreams that I had meant that my marriage was going to fail by means of the old wise tale. It was seven years after my wife passed away that I found out from my brother that my ex-wife passed away. Then I phoned my ex-father-in-law and then he told me that he was a little bit blame for the divorce. My ex-father-in-law said that he should have bought the meat packing place in the small town and got my wife, and I would have worked in the meat packing place and would make good money for that job. Then he said that would be our business when father-in-law would retire, and we got trained. Then my father-in-law said to my wife come back as a fawn and looked at her grave and then disappeared without a trace or a footprint that led nowhere just in circles. The fawn appeared to smell the new grave before disappearing.

It was a few years later my ex-father-in-law phoned me from the hospital. He told me that he was very sick and that his youngest son was with him. Then he said on his death bed to me quite smoking and drinking alcohol. Then he said to me to get remarried and have a family. Then guess what he said? He said to me not to be scared of dying, that everything was in place for me. When it is time for me to go where I am supposed to be. But the funny thing is I never told him that I was scared.

I will never understand how he knew that I had a fear of dying. When he and I talked it was never brought up about death at all. Then I still do not know how he knew that I was scared of dying or who told him that. Maybe an angel or God told him to tell me what will happen.

When my ex-father-in-law passed away, his property was sold. Then his son moved to his sister's place and is living with them for as long as I know. Then there was my ex-fathers-in-law brother that had an accident that cost the sight of his eye. The accident happened when he was doing fencing and a piece of part he was dripping and hit a rock and splint off. Then was rushed to the hospital and removed his eye. Then he had to go to the doctor for six months. Then after six months and everything was healed up, they stuck a glass eye in for him. Then he had at least six more months of visiting the doctor in the city to check for infection.

When I was visiting and dating my vowed to be father-in-law, we would go to the town dump to pick up copper wire and bottles and cows and anything that was worth any money. Then lots of times we would go fishing with the whole family and have a cookout. The cookout was mostly wieners and hamburgers and a salad and pop. The things my father-in-law did in a funny way like make potato wine and champagne and tried to make beer with a beer kit which did not work well. The smell was kind of sickening, like vomiting.

Then about seven years later when I was working in the city, I met a boy, and he said that his dad had just passed away by the means of doing a hoofing job and had a heart attack and fell off the roof and hit his head on a bundle of shingles. The man was in his sixties and a little overweight.

Then about six months later I met the boy's mom and her two daughters. Which the two daughters were on their own when I first meet her. That fall the bot did not want to go to school. Then I took him out to work with me. I told his mom he would be back to school within a month. The boy and I did some hoofing together and it got pretty cold in the mornings. We went to work early to strip the roof off. The boy got pretty cold and decided the school was a lot warmer than outside.

I lived with the boy's mom for about fifteen years until she passed away. We lived in the city and got along as a family. Well. Then also there were an apple tree and plum and cherry trees in the back yard. Then a few years later, she and I bought a new car which was great on fuel. Then about a year and a half we decided to sell the new car. The reason was the boy needed six thousand dollars to go to pay school in Calgary. The boy was taking some kind of computer test, also I put in fifteen hundred dollars to help.

When the weather got cold, I went to work in a scrap yard cutting metal and steel pipes. The crew cut up all week and on Saturday I was called in to help load semi-trucks of steel to go to a recycling place in another city. Then I got a driving job for the same company hauling scrape bins of steel to the yard. I worked there for about two winters there.

Then I worked on my own again and went back roofing and done some metal roofing. Then I got a job doing grain bins for a company. Then I got a job doing a commercial building in the city. The job consisted of removing asbestos and installing metal on the walls. The asbestos was in a solid form and had to be loaded in a covered trailer and hauled out of town to a pit that was dug. I had no masks on or wore no gloves at all. I did not know about the health risk I was taken.

One summer, I had a surprise come my way that I did not know that was going to happen to me. The surprise was that my brother and his wife and son had come to see me and also, they brought our foster father along with them. And I asked where they were and told me they went on a holiday to Disney land and a few other places they went to see. They stayed in the city for a while then they went back home. We had a very good talk and visit that I never seen them for quite a while.

Then later that summer I was working in a small city and my foster pa came to visit and ended up helping me at the trailer building company. The job was to build a storage shop for material like shingles and insulation and paint nails etc... My foster pa stayed until the job was done and then I took him back home and I stayed for the night. The next morning after breakfast went back home. That was the last job foster pa helped me with. Then a few years later he passed away and I was at the funeral.

One time I was doing a job out of town and got home late and then got a phone call to come to work. My co-worker and I left the city at four in the morning to be at work by eight o'clock. The job was to set up a big grain bin for a farmer. It was harvesting time and needed it up fast. It was a ten thousand busher bin with a special floor put into place. My co-worker and I were very tired when we got home. The next week I went to the company for our checks.

Then that summer I did other jobs for that company. Then that winter I went to the big city to go to work as a roofer. That is when I had a few years' experience in that kind of work. Then in the spring I went I went to help a friend out. The friend had a TS fourteen and what was needed was to build an oil lease for an oil company. Then after that job was done, I did fencing for him. Then works for his neighbor doing irrigation moves.

That fall when the crops were off, I went to work for a few farm machinery places. Some jobs consisted of putting cultivator together and grain elevators and cloaks on tractors. I had one accident that happened. That was a wrench slipped and skinned my baby finger. I will always have that fear for the rest of my life.

Late that fall I went back to roofing in the city that paid very well. I ended up working until two days before Christmas then headed home. Then when I was working in the city, I loaded the half ton too heavy and broke an axle on the way to the dump. The next day I phoned a tow truck and had a garage put a new axle in then hit for the dump and unloaded. That year was very good because I was busy and got paid very well. My gross income for that year was sixty thousand dollars before expenses. I had to pay dump fees and gas for the truck and oil for the gun and new hoses and air compressor repair.

One year my common law wife helps me do some roofing. Then one time I showed her how to cut the ridge cap and I went back on the roof. Then about half an hour I checked on her and she had cut the ridge cap backwards, so they were no good. So, I showed her again and she got it right. Then one day she came onto the roof with me and helped me strip the roof and clean it up before shining it. I showed her how to use the air nailer and then she pointed the gun at me and told her it was not a toy, and I passed the gun away from my face. Then a nail shot out and headache off me teethy and cut my top lip.

After a few years my common law wife decided to sell the house. The reason was she was very sick and could not keep up with the lawn care. Then the stairs were getting to her also. Once she found out she had cancer she just gave up on life because it was a n0n-winning battle. She was taking a lot of different kinds of medicine for her pain.

Then after fifteen years of common law, we decided to split up and she moved to her daughter's place in the big city. About a month after she moved to her daughter's place, they went to see a doctor at the hospital. Then on the way back they had an accident. Someone hit the back of her daughter's car. Then there

was the hard hit which caused whip lash. Not only whip lash but broke her mom's neck. They were rushed back to the hospital, and they put a neck brace on her mom. When they got out of the hospital her daughter phoned me. What was said was that her mom only had about five or six weeks to live, and I was supposed to come and see her. Then I was working on the pipeline company, and I was going to the big city on the weekend when I had day off.

Then I got a phone call the next morning from my common law's daughter. The news was not good, she had passed away that night in bed with her daughter and son by her side. It was just too late for me to say goodbye to her and give her a kiss. My common law wife told her daughter there was a box she made up for me but never got it, I was a pallbearer for her funeral.

Then getting back, a few years earlier when we owned the house. There was a little thing that happened like her mom on night decided to go for a walk and never showed up. Then her dad phoned and asked if we could find her. Then we went the night away and found her about a block away and lost. By the way she had Alzheimer's disease. Then time for the nursing home whenever dad passed away and six months later her mom passed away.

Then one day I phoned up my uncle to see how he was doing. I had been busy and kind of forgot about the family. Anyway, my auntie answered the phone and said that my uncle had passed away seven years ago. But I did not think it was that long I talked to him. Uncle was the bary on dad's side and the last one to leave the earth for a better place.

My uncle was the one that built a new house on the homestead. Then each year he went out hunting deer and prairie chickens and was successful. Hunting is always fun in our family like playing golf for other folks. Then also when the homestead life was over our trapping and snaring was also over. That as one thing that was missed out hunting dog our duck hunting and making ice cream.

Then the old days are gone, and the new day begins when you wake up in the morning. Remember the old days as a lesson to be learned. You never know what tomorrow will bring for you. There was a lot of stuff to talk about, but I will do a little summary for all of you in our big family.

SUMMARY

Life is short and when you are young you can hardly wait until you grow up. Then when you grow up, life is in the fast pages.

Then after thirty-five years of being single we decided to get married. It will be like a new world all over again. I have been with the beautiful lady for four years and have known her for the last ten years. We are talking about the east coast to spend our last day up there in a log cabin beside the lake.

I hope everyone knows where we come from when you read the story. One thing for sure is we will meet again in heaven and just maybe before just once by chance. I love the whole family. This is ninety percent of my life I told.

SEE YOU SOMETIME

THE END

WHAT TRUE LOVE MEANS

I am writing this what a man and a lady goes through in ((Life)). This is ALBERT BABCOCK telling about a young lady named DEANNA MARIE KATHLEEN POWER.

Deanna and I, Albert Babcock meet in medicine hat Alberta about 10 years ago. When Deanna was walking down the street, she was asking God for her guardian angel. At that time, I was walking down the same street when we bumped into each other. Deanna and I met about one year before through a friend other. Anyway, Deanna asked me to come up to her place for a beer or a coffee whichever I wanted. And talked all night long a decided to spend Christmas together. We were both happy to spend time together.

About six months later we separated for about three years. Then one day the same thing happened again. Deanna was walking down the street sad about something and again asking God for her guardian angel and of course I was there again, but on a different street. Then I asked her to come up and see my apartment, then we had coffee, had no beer then.

Then I asked her if she wanted to stay with me and look after my apartment while I was at work in Fort McMurray.

Deanna said she would be happy to look after my place while I was gone to work. Then when I got home from work Deanna, and I started dating. Then she asked if she could stay permanently with me, and I said yes pf course you can.

The second trip from work, Deanna started telling me stories about her growing up. The one that stood out the most was the one when she started playing the piano. Deanna just sat down and started playing the piano. When her dad came home from work and heard the piano being played. Then her dad asked her mom who was playing piano. Her mom said it was Deanna.

Deanna had a big heart, so big if you need a tonnie for coffee she would give it to you. Deanna would help so-called friends that used her kindness. If Deanna needed help, they were not there for her. I was the one that was there for her seven days a week twenty-four hours a day.

Deanna and I made a few small trips, one was to a lake where she took her boys. I mean her son sat. Deanna loved camping sleeping in the tent especially when it rained out.

One of Deanna's favorite things were to go fishing and another was to play musical instrument and sing her favorite song by Patsy Cline songs Crazy plus many other songs.

Deanna was musical inclined in singing and playing piano, cord organ, the spoons, which was learned from her dad and guitar and her harmonica.

Deanna told me a story about her dad and her. The story was that her dad and her went on a snow mobile and a bob sleigh to get a load of wood for their cabin. They came across the creek and her dad told Deanna to hold on, that they were going up a hill.

Her dad speeds up to make it to the top of the hill where the cabin was. Deanna likes going hunting with her dad when they went moose hunting and fishing. Deanna likes outdoors sports, when possible, she likes hanging out with her dad. Deanna's dad was her favorite of all the family then her grandparents.

Deanna never liked being alone, always someone with her. Never sleeping alone would always get out of bed and sleep with her sister. She loved her brothers also.

When Deanna would go to visit her grandparents. The grandfather would tease grandmother that here comes cookie. Then grandmother would say she is not a cookie she is a power girl.

SUMMARY

Deanna had planned to marry Albert in NEWFOUNDLAND. Shortly after we got there and was supposed to be at her sister's place. The reason Deanna loved Albert was he's older than her. Deanna loved older men to take care of her and love her as a human being. Albert was the lucky one to spend the time with a fine lady as she was.

Deanna was so much in love with Albert that up to her last days. Deanna wants Albert to retire and spend the last of our lives together at home. Deanna asks Albert to quit work for a year to be together until she passes away. Which Albert was beside her until the end. Deanna wants to babysit her granddaughter in the worse way. First grandchild.

Deanna Said the two youngest kids would find us in NEWFOUND LAND.

This is in the memory of DEANNA MARIE KATHLEEN POWER. Everyone knew her, will miss her but still in our hearts.

Appendix

In Memory of the Babcock Family